When the Heart Zooms In

When the Heart Zooms In

Notes for Quotes

F. ARISANDY

RESOURCE *Publications* · Eugene, Oregon

WHEN THE HEART ZOOMS IN
Notes for Quotes

Resource Publications
An Imprint of Wipf and Stock Publishers
199 W. 8th Ave., Suite 3
Eugene, OR 97401

www.wipfandstock.com

PAPERBACK ISBN: 978-1-6667-6209-9
HARDCOVER ISBN: 978-1-6667-6210-5
EBOOK ISBN: 978-1-6667-6211-2

11/10/22

This book is dedicated to those who are dealing with their mental health, gender identity, expressivism, and social justice; those who are struggling for their choice, joy, and love. Special mentions are given to my fellow refugees, immigrants, sojourners, and human trafficking survivors.

We can stumble. Get up and carry on walking! You will get closer to the bright end of the long cave.

Your purpose in life is to find your purpose and give your whole heart and soul to it.

—BUDDHA

Contents

A note from the author

When the Heart Zooms in: Notes for Quotes is a poetry book about my personal journeys across three places: Indonesia, Malaysia, and the United States, that always touch my deepest heart. The title represents how I look at specific things in a deeper way to focus, which involves multi-facets of feelings that I express in each poem, such as sadness and happiness, disappointment and optimism, beast and beauty, and hopelessness and hopefulness. All of these feelings cover various topics, which are mostly about places, nature, gender, affection, and mental health. This poetry is very personal yet, well deserved to be shared with people to promote expressivism and mental health. There are 55 poems in this book using the five senses with a heart and horizons.

As a non-native English speaker, I composed this book with more frequent English words so that it will be easier for people who speak English as a second language to understand. This book is also personal but authentic, which means I share my experience and life with people based on the real deal. I hope poetry can be like music lyrics that are universal and authentic so that people who read this book can relate the poems to their lives and experiences through their senses, hearts, and minds.

As my first poetry publication, this book may not be perfect. Therefore, I would gladly accept any input for my future publication as I want this book to be the milestone of my future poetry books.

F. Arisandy

Alien

Feet do not understand,
Heart speaks up
Mind never stops working
I force my feet to follow the louder

A land of new things
I feel stranded and lost
Am I closing my eyes?
Tear's streaming down
I am sad

The lady with wrinkles and old veils
Who used to smile at me
The gentleman with pearls of wisdom
Who used to forge me

Now, my mind is the only survivor
I let my brain lead the way
Because I believe in sunshine
Tomorrow will come and shine
My path

America

A child listens to the song
He witnesses the dance
He might admire the singer
With her blond hair and brown eyes
He sees deeper into the scenery

His mom comes with a puzzle in mind
She could believe in her mind
Her son falls in love in the morning
She is paused for a question
The kid challenges her
She says "beauty"

The beauty of attractions
The beauty of promises
The beauty of hopes
The kid's eyes shine
Like a glass window in the rain

Nobody understands his spark of mind
He speaks to himself to never let her go
He falls in love earlier indeed
He writes in a skyline
Praying to the skies above
He sees an air car
He wants to go there

He wants to hold her tightly
And states his love to her, America

The kid is me

Belitung

A little dot on the world map
A lot of stories on the mind map
I am drowned in the sea of nowhere
Life can be a prison
Steps are caught

A bird that has wings can't fly
It is not because they are too small
It is because they are tied
I prefer to stay
To accept the truth
To learn about the beauty

The island is where beautiful flowers blossom
Where the waves chase the coastline
My feet touch its beautiful snowy sand
Heart feels graced by Lord

Stopwatch keeps counting
Hair misses its previous boldness
Lines start to draw the outer layer
Neurons argue about setting free
The future is ours to see

Bohemian Rhapsody

Fingers dance on the strings
Beats compete with the emotional heart
Sounds penetrate the shields in the snail couple
My mind is blown away

The verses reflect the scream of instinct
I can hear the indefinite despair
The emotion feels like protesting God's
Eyes cannot be a well of feelings
Heart explodes the time bomb

Mamas, if only we could decide our birth
Poor kids would prefer not to be born
You cry for us
We cry for you harder
You deserve all the love
And happiness in the world
You used to say "be strong"
Please be strong inside
Your tears worth The Red Beryl

Everything has been set that way
Embrace the reality
Run the life
Years will be fine
Without me

Cinta Pertama (First Love)

An entity comes unpredictably
An entity creates my sleepless nights
Worries and fears limit the feelings
I may be crazy

The brightest star is so beautiful to see
I can't touch it in this state
Should I fly to get you?
It seems impossible

The distance between us is real
My shine is not as bright as yours
You can't even see me
I feel so small and powerless

I wish a wormhole appeared
That will take me to you
I can only wake up from my sleep
Find that the life is real to face

I will save it for good
A teenage dream is always cruel
It brings such a wild fantasy
About someone loved who hits the heart

COVID-19

The sparkling of pine trees still echoes
The Lady Eve would arrive soon
A market abroad sounds louder
Do buyers crowd for their bellies?

My eyes speak louder than my thoughts
TV cannot stop talking about you
I am lost in my confusion
What happens to this world?

The world has sounded so talkative
You shut it up with force without mercy
You show your true arrogance over choices
You hate us

Our despair has led us to spectrum
We realize that you came for a reason
God pities our Mother Earth
The skies let the sunshine through now

The protons in our head want to make a peace
No more blaming each other
Can we live side to side?
You can be close to me
but you can't take me

Desk

Your clothes are made from papers
I give you pens as your earrings
You save books in your pocket
You hold my laptop for me

You seem happy
You show your strength
You're always ready
But you can't hide your age

I see wrinkles on your face
I know you can't stand well
Your bones are fragile
The joints are saggy

What can I do to repay you?
A friend should never forget his best friend
I don't want to let you go in these conditions
I would never let you down

I realize you'll say goodbye to me
You know your time will be over
There isn't enough time
You'll beg for my pardon

Desk,
You have to know
That you'll always have the space
In my heart and home
No matter what happens to you

Destiny

Face of happiness
Heart of sadness
I meet lessons
I have blessings

Something that I never know
Lessons that sometimes I can't learn
I feel like walking on the long road
Heading to the unknown

I see stars at night guarding the moon
I admire the sun coloring the skies
I never know if tomorrow will be today
I just know that I don't know

My mind thinks so hard
About the place that I will come at
I just can dream of a paradise
But I just know that I don't know

Bump me with a party and laughter
Bake me cakes and bread
Bathe me with pillows and a soft blanket
Bring me love and affection

Eclipse

The full moon can be the night sun to see
The moon turns scythe when it's tired
The stars become the spotlights
They ornament the darkness

On the night of the loss of Lady Moon
Another lady was working on her womb
She had no ideas about her own life
She let an existence ruin her from the inside

A boy cried out loud
He didn't feel really sad
It was the only thing he could
He felt thankful to the universe

Two ladies came to success
They looked so blissful
The sounds of a city were heard
The euphoria is the evidence of love

English

I did not understand you
When you first arrived
I even thought that I didn't need to know you
I ignored you

You came again through waves
Wanting me to get you
This time I could not ignore you
As you appeared with all I wanted

I knew I needed you
Still, I could not accept you easily
I asked my parents for letting you in
They said yes to your attraction

I learned about you
I listened to you through the angelic voices
You made me fall in love
You sit right beside my Mother tongue

My mouth is not only for life
It is for expressing my mind
To all people with different colors
To all people with different minds

You have experiences with me
You extend my horizons
You meet me with friends
You give me my food

FNU

Sheets of a book come to my hand
He sees his reflection on the first page
His fingers try to move to another page
They are looking for another reflection

Right in the place, the eyes spot their target
They see a man with a beard and without his glasses
They pause on a machine product
A new name sounds so strange to him
He has a question about whose it is
His fingers dance on a screen
They want to find out a light
Eyes spot it and send it to the brain
It is a new name for an alien in a country

One is always good but two is always better
The loneliness of a name comes to an end
Should I feel happy about that?
Or should I blame my parents for that?
First name unknown is a fact of an unknown mind

Flamboyan

Afternoons always seem so exciting
Kids are really into playing with you
Two wear shorts
One eats snacks
Mothers talk about many issues

A girl draws some lines
Three others prepare the stones
The rule is set
They are ready to play

Two girls with in-line skates chase each other
One falls and cries
Her mother blames her
She cries even louder
They leave

The sun sets right on the horizon
More motorcycles and cars pass
Doors open, and voices resonate to call people back
The day is done right in the street of Flamboyan

Georgia 1

The sun comes out from his hiding
The time clocks at 07.20 am
The bird stops her long journey
Bringing out the lice from their hiding

People form a snake line
One by one is called
They come to judgment
Whether their dream should be kept

Five wet fingers try hard to see
They put on a white flag
They know they'll win when they give up
The heartbeat stops running

Three boxes await their destiny
They seem to follow their master
One is stopped for mother's love
It is supposed to let the love go

The fast worm moves the body
Bringing him to a nest of birds
Where he can feel his blood free from the waterfall
It's time to say goodbye to the hut of judgment
Atlanta, Georgia

Georgia 2

The eyes stumble on a line of words
The news widens the lids
The brain can't believe it
The heart breaks at sudden

Women who work for life
Their minds know nothing about politics
Their hearts that believe in human's love
Have been betrayed without vengeance

Their families fall into pieces
The kids' fates hang in imbalance
They don't know how to replace the souls
They can't cry as the tears have been dry
The scars are too deep to knit

People can't ever choose their skins
I can't choose my eye shape
My body is not my wish
I know hate just poisons my heart
I will never let it conquer my love
We must realize that we're here
Because of love
For God's love
So please more love

Hollywood

I can see you from the distance
You look prominent among the others
You wave to all people as if you invite them
Hollywood Sign, you're the king on the throne

Steps of people are beautiful to see
They walk slowly to see the walk
Stars are close to see
They shine along the way
Walk of Fame, you're the red carpet

Voices and sounds can be heard so clearly
They resonate with the world
People act to be someone else
They seem to enjoy the roles
Hollywood's music and movies, you're the epicenter of the world

Palm trees still can be seen in their disguise
Skyscrapers defeat the stars
The lights replace the sun
Humans forget the darkness
Hollywood at night is the moon of the skies

History

They always say "Forget about the past"
People should live for today
And they dream for tomorrow
That's a perfect design

I drive to the destination
I focus on the signs on the road to keep me safe
But I need to see the mirrors to look back for the safety
I cannot forget the backward to be forward

I recall all the bad and good things in life
It does not mean I cannot move on
It's because I need them to live on

History. . . You make us what we are now
You give us lessons to learn
Lessons to live up the life
We can't ever leave you behind
Because you feed our mind for being able to walk

/

I who stare at the skies
I who miss the summer
I who smell the beach
I who love the earth

I live for love
I smile for goodness
I laugh for jokes
I dream for happiness

I cry for hurt
I hate for betrayal
I hide for fakeness
I wake for nightmare

I am strong outside
I am fragile inside
I am ambitious about things
I am caring about things

I am

Indonesia

God lets me fall into you
I wake up for the first time in you
I lay my body on you
I breathe your air

The islands are blessings
That I can never explore all
The coconut trees wave to the sea
They invite the waves to touch their feet

People dance for Gods
I dance for the people
People sing for nature
I sing for the people

Pepper, cumin, and cinnamon that people admire
They come for this source of wealth
I thank them for the rich taste on my tongue
That I always satisfy my greed

I hear people speak
I read people write
I use your tongue to tell my mind
I recall your esthetic to writing my poem

I may be away from you

I could start my new love
But I will not forget about you
The blood runs through my heart
It will always belong to you
Indonesia

In mind

Distance matters
Eyes have limits to see
Ears receive limited waves
Minds wander without borders

I can see what eyes can't see
I can see even in my sleep
The views
The fears
The nonsense

A strong body becomes fragile
When it comes to mind
A weak body becomes independent
When it comes to mind
An ordinary body becomes eye-opening
When it comes to mind

Mind can stop the tears
Mind can stop the fears
Mind can change your nature
Mind can change your future
It's all in your mind

Jakarta

Night still exists
The spacious place seems unfamiliar
People there look like me
I am stranded in my own homeland

I sleep on the chair
Waiting for the sun to grow
I wake up to see the strange view in-depth
I decide to leave

The buildings seem to claw the sky
There's no more blue on it
Motors fart and become arrogant
My nose is killed when it accepts the truth

People look like people but not
They don't see me
Even their eyes don't want to move
I'm invisible in my visible
I keep telling myself that everything's alright
They just need a happy life
They just need to be taught to care

Jakarta in mind

Jasmines

Fairness is your skin
The color that never gives up on snow
You show that you're pure and flawless
You're just who you are

Propeller is the shape of you
As if you want to turn all the wind
Your moles are your beauty marks
That are comparable to Marilyn Monroe

Your body scent is as strong as your body
You invite flying cops to approach
Humans can never stop adoring you
They're jealous of your scent
Yet you never stop helping them
I see you in my morning cup
Giving me a touch of peace
I see you in the bride's crown
Showing people that you're noble

Jasmine, the flower of powers

K-6

I didn't care about how much I can earn
I had nowhere I will take my last breath
I was blind with whom I will marry
I did love who they are

Mother is his favorite word
A young boy liked the balls
His massive beliefs grew for his friends
But, he seemed unhappy with his school

English was absent
Math haunted his days
Religion was preaching
Arts became his siblings

My teachers who look like my gods
I listened to them more than my president
They managed my time
They could judge what I worked so hard
They showed me that parents do not always spoil

I tried not to be sad
I steeled my heart from nervousness
My anger was not allowed to see
The disappointment should have been awhile

You teach me to grow through suffering

Kent State University

Blue calms me like the ocean
You drown me in you
I am immersed in knowledge
The knowledge feeds my brain
My medal is gold as you wish

Flashes strike me in no rains
I am so full of power
The power to put my head up when the rain pours
A source that charges my battery when I'm weak
You revive my spirit

Squirrels captivate me
I chase you for something
Something about my beautiful dream
I see who I am in the future
A person who shares the beauty of life with people

Eagles fly so high above me
They grab me up so fast
Taking me to feel the air of change
Making me learn how to spread my wings
Flying to a place where I can make my nest

You are what a passion really is

Malaysia

A brother that sits beside us
He is not far but may feel far
When the heart falls into doubts
About our chemistry
Our blood is not a question
Our hearts question many things
You'll always be there when we're down
Does your heart just wonder about the cause?
You react differently when we're up
Does your heart envy our little walk?
We argue about humans
We scramble over the pillows
But we struggle for our oil
You're not our friend
You're more than that
Brother is still brother
No matter how hard our times are
Deep in our hearts, we know
That we have the romance
That we grow a care
That we call each other when we're quite

Brother Malaysia

Malaysia 2

19 is the number on my cake
Being in the whale to go somewhere
Escaping from how sad it is
The disc in my mind still remembers her tears
Letting a light green leaf drift

Feet touch the land
His eyes are confused about things
Getting a new image of new sights
He surrenders his life into the vast land

In distance, he sees a big ship on land
The ship that may pay him for life
Their eyes spot a little man
He knows he would be eaten by their arrogance
Yet, his hunger is bigger than his anger

I wink at people and vomit for myself
My stay runs with lightspeed into my leave
A year at a glance

May 4th

The sun blinds the eyes
The clouds move away
The blue sky stretches out
The trees grow their hair and nails
Spring turns to Fall at sudden
No more celebrations
No more plans
There's just silence of nature
Seeing humans lose their humans
Kent State cries
United States regrets
Earth state pauses
On the day of 4, on the death of 4
What do you want now?
Young warriors have been defeated
In the unfair nonsense
Don't you feel ashamed of the grasses?
That always keep their babies safe
That always give space to their fellows
The tragedy makes us confused about the term "human"
As heart and brain that we're proud of do not exist
If humans should kill the other humans
I question God why we are born to die

The four souls can never be the four breezes
Their names are not carved on the sand
To be wiped away by the waves
They are carved on the rock to stay forever
Rest in spirit, we'll never stop

Mother

Mother, how are you today?
A chunk that I always say to you
The years have separated us
The times have limited us
I still remember the tears you share with me
The ward keeps your silence
The wand keeps my knowledge

I did try to be the best for you
I am sorry for my decision
I leave you for what I want
I know you are hurt

My lips want you to know
That my tears drop
Right after my head turns from you
What I want is what I want you to be
I want your health
I cheer for your happiness
Even, when we stop sharing the same air to breathe
and start sharing the disappointments

Words can never describe how big my love to you is
I can't ever repay you, even with the sea of diamonds
I just can thank you
For the sweat you've dropped

MOTHER

For the nights you've sacrificed
I thank you for never giving me up on me
The love seems to be real
You're far in my eyes
But you're so close to my heart
Happy Mother's Day

Mother Tongue, An Ode to

Mother,
One of the most emotional words
I've heard you since I wasn't born
I've listened to many beautiful words
I speak up about my ears, eyes, brain, and heart
I was blind
To see the wonderous horizon
You let my eyes work with my organs
My fingers are not only to touch
I use them to express
I want to thank you for your coming
All you have provided me
You are my first love
And you will always be inside of me
Thank you, Mother Tongue

My First Broken Heart

Dear Mom,
Let me have your shoulder

I've never felt this pain before
When I was a kid, you used to tell me
The stories about the beauty of this world
I run for my life optimistically and heartfully
Wishing the stories were real for me
The more number I get, the more I realize
That more bitterness and lessons I meet
Feeling the failure when I am feeling the sweetness
Feeling the loss when I am starting the beliefs
"I love you" is not only said for love
It is also for the farewell
I realize all you did was to strengthen me
It's just life that can be so cruel

Love could not be seen
Now I see it in you

Nervousness

You come at sudden
Taking out all the plans
Rip out all the joy
Giving a taste of failure

Your biggest enemy is a man called "confidence"
You're always forgotten by him
You despise him like cats hate dogs
You'll always battle with him
For conquering what I believe

Some say you're normal and good
You're the proof of the existence of responsibility
You can make me think about how far I've gone
But should you always ripple my heart?

I'm not scared of you
This is me
I believe in steel heart
There's no room for you

Niagara Falls

Glasses flow
Running for a new experience
The excitement becomes greater
Being close to the basket hole

Skyscrapers try to show up their heights
Blocking the sunlight to touch the skin
Even eyes have no time to blink
Winked by the beauty of the underworld

The voices of people want to defeat theirs
They say: "I am your mother. You live on me."
But the faces of smiles explaining sparkling hearts
Seem beautiful to see like you

Rainbows are not only a make-up for the sky
I can see the colors beautify the sky down there
Creating its new wonderous place
Telling that being up is not being exclusive

The sun needs to rest
Now, his children need to be independent
Lights shoot the falls
Creating another beauty for never-satisfied eyes

Nokia

Hands hold you tight
Fingers touch your toes
Addiction is real
It's not easy for you to release
Who's wrong?
You're so captivating
Full of attractions of all new
You are destined to be my company
I say good night before my sleep
I say good morning when I wake up
My world seems drawn to you
You are my secret love
Taking you wherever I go
Holding you whenever I want
How can I forget about the good old times?
You've saved all of my stories
The first is always memorable
My old friend
Nokia

Onion

I cry but I don't have the wounds
You challenge me through your smell
You hate me for putting the cut on you
My eyes can't stop the pain
As if you want to share the pain you feel with me

You have to know that I love you
You're just to die for
Even when you're angry
My love is bigger than my hate

You are part of my body
Years of being with you are never boring
I'm addicted to you
More than the white cloves
They say you're so sweet but sad
Nothing comes easy
Just believe that everything hard
Will bring sweetness in the end

Palembang, My Home

Two twins become the rope of two different sisters
The calm flow of yellow liquid meets their needs
Houses spread from the center to the edges
People seem to enjoy the ups and downs

When Mr. Light shines you to the fullest
I can see the real face of who you are
You look full of settlers and their ornaments
You may seem tired of them

Twilight awaits you in the distance
He can't wait to take you to your bed
To whisper Mrs. Beauty to prepare
To tell the birds to sing their best songs

Now, the blue horizon has gone
Letting you forget about the hard job
Making you feel the meaning of serenity
Sleep soundly even for awhile
Because your children need you
When morning comes

Persian Cat, The

I spot you in the distance
Stunned by your look
Amazed by your attitude
Wishing you are mine

The future is not ours to hold
It may bring you something you never dream
It could entrust you to something you already expect
Now, my hands can hold you

Your gray hair does not mean your ages
It defines your beauty
It shows God's goodness
When your tongue is tired
My hand will help you out

Friendship is not only about humanity
I find you my bestie
Always feel sad when I leave
Always look glad when I live
Thank you for the memories
Rest in happiness, Momo
Till we meet again

Quail

One morning, you cry
They look at you arrogantly
Thinking that they have mastered you
Forgetting that I have mastered them

I chase for you
Trying to make you believe
My foot walks slowly
My hands want to hold you

An open is a shock to see
Mother Nature makes the rules
I can't believe the law
I believe what I feel

Your pain is not to see
Your eyes turn dim
You show the weak body
You speak to me for my mercy

Keeping you safe is my nature
The nature that emerges in affection
A creature who experiences pain
A creature who has an eye in his heart

Quay of Tanjung Kelayang Beach

A man sitting heading to the door of the sun
Old wooden planks cry when people step
Letting his ears hear the sounds of gravity
He is too calm to make a move of his body
He enjoys the orange on the skylines

His mind keeps wanting the peace to stay
People's voices are nothing compared to the birds'
Compared to the small moves of the sea
He becomes a baby who sleeps in his mother's arms
That he always misses happening in his life

The nuance just leaves him behind
But it leaves him in the full mind
He has to say goodbye to this peace
He promises the quay to be back again
He will

Quit

Nights don't feel the same
Mind never stops babbling
Love becomes doubt
Mom's words seem louder
Telling how my mind should act
Forcing how my feet can walk
A place where I see beautiful souls
A clock where time seems to fleet
The seat that always lifts me up
The desk that always holds me up
How can I forget about their merits?
Heart has been made up
We don't always get what we want
Making the lady happy is another merit
I walk my way out
Looking straight to the street out
Future, please be kind to me
I quit

Rain

Tears of the skies
For sadness
For happiness
For goodness
For bitterness

You cry at the pale bodies in their best outfits
As if you just can't let them go
Or you just feel emphatic for their family
We know you cry for our weaknesses

A bright Sunday walks in
He invites me to go out
To see the beauty of God's mind
I see the skies want to cry
They want happiness too
Just let them cry for some ticks
Their tears of joy

The land looks deeply wounded
Grass loses its color
Fish start to overthink things
All lives pray to the skies above
Until He answers the melody of wishes
He can't hold it any longer

He cries for His kids' sufferings
He forgives us through his drops

Our brain is too young to forget her
We choose to close our eyes when we can see
She is the one who is always low-profiled
Her eyes closed tightly when she needs to scold
Water seems so kind shows her strength
Forgive us to forget you
We confess our weak bodies
Stop your anger, Mother Nature
We promise that we always remember you
We are so small to fight against your little sweat

Rainbow

After darkness, brightness appears slowly
After cry, smile stretches out
After rain, earth wipes her face
She puts some colorful make on it

All the emotions of yours become a line
All I can see is the beauty of a stairway
Your happiness in red
Your joy and celebration in yellow
Your new hope in green
Your mystery and silence in blue
Your energy and power in orange

I wish I could see the angels from heaven
Coming down to earth for their short visit
The bridge of beauty is their timekeeper
You start to fade away to call them back
They run so quickly without wanting to stay
The bridge of heaven that people wish to walk on
Heading to immortal love and happiness

Ramadan

A tiny light appears in her dim
That watery eyes can't see barely
The moon is your symbol
The symbol of new special days

The month is your name
The 9th child of 12 siblings
Your parents name you a "burning heat"
The heat that purifies my dirty soul
Greediness is my daily diet
Lust is my biggest thirst
Anger is my instant way out
Hatred is my interest
You teach me to let all fake happiness go
It is not the chain that handcuffs
It's the poison in your heart
True freedom means a peaceful heart
When we close our eyes for good

The leftovers fill out the bag
Only squirrels wish to taste
People prefer to die in hunger
Their dignity seems more important

A month lets me taste the suffering

A month makes me cry for the suffering

A month defines me the meaning of thanks

Ramadan, the month of empathy

30 days of lessons of this temporary life

At the end of the day, we only have the merits

The holiness is not you

It is our hearts

Ramadan Kareem

Siblings, my

Four is all about us
An even number against all the odds
The bed is the witness
We share with each other
We kick out each other
We laugh at each other
We cry at each other
Many stories in a small pile of cotton

The food has never been ours
We share us bless
The jokes mean the bonds
The bonds exceed the blood

We forget about the togetherness
We let the distance limit the bond
We fight for our emotions
We separate for the gold

Brother, sisters
How I miss the times
Please never forget the sweet bitterness
How hard it is
We're siblings

We live, we laugh, we love

Soul

Blood runs so fast
Heart beats like a drum
Eyes turn red
Mouth seems trembling
Pores pump the water out
Lungs sound so short
Ears are so sensitive
Feet can never stand tall
Hands feel so cold
Intestines become numb
Hair heads to the north
Nails lose their true color
Teeth push each other

The time I realize
It's not my body that controls
My soul speaks

To Those Who Are So Far Away

You leave me behind
Without saying good night
The faces aren't clear to see
No emotions can be felt
You sleep so tight
Do you want me to envy you?
Yes, you do!
I am jealous you've moved on from me

The white clothes cover the white body
My tears drop for you who don't cry for me
It's not fair if you don't feel this pain
I want you to see how I live
Without the ones that I love
You're free while I'm tied
You forget the things while I forge the things

To those who are so far away
I send you my hello
I know you know my regrets
I hope for my apology
Let me see you one more time
In my sleep

Umbrella

Flowers blossom after a rain
You blossom in the middle of the rain
Because you do it for people in need
You seem like a shelter that can move

I know how hard the drops hit you
Millions of niddles from the sky are merciless
Sometimes you hang imbalance
When He blows the air like celebrating His birthday

You say "Please hang on. I can take it."
I feel my face rains giving me the sense of seawater
I'm holding you tight because I believe in you
You will never leave me alone in this storm

One of your bones sounds to crack
I hold you up as strongly as I can
I hope now you can hang on
I'll fix you soon after we make it through

Our house door wants to know our story
He just can let us go in speechlessly
There's nothing I could explain
But I can say you're my savior

Vivid

Time is just about a number on a calendar
We never know what it brings in the future
But I know where it brought me yesterday
The memories of old friends are still vivid
I still have their frame hanging on the wall of my mind
Their teeth are not shy to show up their color
The lungs push the air hard through the two cords
They speak their feelings out loud
The old memories are still vivid
When a bond needs to cut itself for the separation
We know that the abstract bond can never be broken
As our hearts build the towers of love to connect us
The vivid memories will always bring our eyes to play
Because there is something that can never go away
The tree of friendship that we plant will let the air meet us
Someday. . . Our new faces are vivid

We Are Who We Are

We were born sick
We can never get healed
We don't need the remedies
We are more than the world thinks

They say there are only two sides to a coin
They say there are only Adam and Eve
We see the ring on the edges of a coin
We see us between Adam and Eve

The fact is the truth
We can't hide who we are
You can't hide who we are
We see through our eyes
You see through your eyes
We hear through our ears
You hear through your ears
And, you speak through your mind
But, we speak through our hearts

The cruelest spit always wants to dissolve us
The sharpest words always want to cut us down
We can't give up as God never gives up
His love is what we believe

You can't turn from your sights

We exist

We were born this way

We are who we are, my LGBTQ community

What's Up?

In the distance of my memory, I could still see you
The old man that may be shy to see me
Or I may be too scary to be seen
One thing is that you're not my nightmare
It's a dream that always haunts me every night
Remembering our good old days
Like a story of an eternal relationship
We forget that clock has walked in its circle many times
Until we need to say goodbye to each other
Life isn't about immortality and consistency
It is about embracing the reality
Because an ideal world doesn't exist
But, is it wrong to remember you?
I miss you like a child misses his doll
You may disappear from my eye plays
Your face will never fade away from my brain
You are the one that my childhood is all about

What a World!

A world that seems intelligent but feels uncivilized
A world that seems caring but feels ignored
A world that seems diligent but feels lazy
A world that seems loving but feels hateful
A world that seems humanist but feels cannibal
A world that seems safe but feels harmful
A world that seems moralistic but feels cruel
A world that seems sacred but feels profane
A world that seems understanding but feels selfish
A world that seems humid but feels drained
A world that seems clean but feels trashy
A world that seems colorful but feels monochrome
A world that seems well but feels sick

A world that seems tough outside but feels thin inside
I stand on

Windows of the World

Piles of wooden sheets in each of you
Giving you different body size
I see some look old and dull
The ones on the table still look fresh

Your thoughts are so wonderous
Traveling the world ain't important to do anymore
I have the magic door of Doraemon in you
Taking me to worlds of different horizons

You light the dark world up
Leaving your eternal flame on it
If eyes are the windows of the heart
You're the windows of the world
An infinity right in my hands
My books are

Xelograph

A woman engraves on a tender wood
She looks happy to make a storyline
A man that she's been waiting for
Time becomes shorter each day

She holds a pencil to draw an image
She writes her message beautifully
She prays while she dances a chisel
She smiles on the surface with imagination
She puts too much hope without logic

My ego fights with hers
My emotions respond to hers
My walk competes against hers
My lips talk about hers

My face reflects hers
Her love exceeds mine
I am her Xelograph

Year, A

I stop at sudden
I wonder what's going on
I am confused about the words
I decide to go home for the answers

The world stops rotating in a minute
No more hectic moves can be seen
No more talkative voices can be heard
Homes that used to miss their dwellers
Have got them back and seem busier

To hide, we ain't in a war
To hibernate, we ain't in a winter
To hush, we ain't in a night
To heal, we ain't in a hospital

Each hour takes considerations
Each day takes prudence
Each week takes patience
Each month takes questions

A year that looks short
A year that looks solid
A year that ain't sharp
The year of 2020

Young

Eyes become wild
Heart feels emotional
Mind crawls curiously
Feet walk so far

What I see is what I believe
To spot every inch of a fake world
My image emerges from the eyes
I'm mistaken

My heart always says good things
To trust each feeling of a fake world
My ideology grows from my emotions
I'm mistaken

I think my brain is the smartest
To answer each question of a fake world
My perception sparks from my nerves
I'm mistaken

Some say walk your miles to wander
To learn each lesson of a fake world
My wisdom blooms from my journeys
I'm right

Yours in mine

It is so fast
It is so illogical
We both know
That not everything can be explained
Through our minds
The two hearts that want to meet
We don't understand the power
They act knowing every feeling in them
Yet, they can't explain

Your smile fissures in the face
Pushing your fair cheeks away
When your heart wants to show up
You show me what I can't feel

Your voice feels so soft and calm
Resonating from your dancing lips
When your heart wants to speak up
You whisper to me, what I can't hear

Your sight tells me the mystery
Glowing from your ocean eyes
When your heart wants to light up
You enlighten me what I can't believe

Your heart in mine

Zoom

Eyes have limits
People are too far to see
Looking at their pictures adds to the longing
To imagine is the only way
Yet not every inch of you can be recalled
Some good memories have been forgotten
My brain has limits

We are caged for the crown troops
Health is more crucial than meeting
Yet, we are too social to confess it
We need our family, teachers, and friends
We can't live without them

Fingers dance on the blocks
They wonder if they find the magic
A word with the last letter in front calls
Touch is made
Teardrops are drops of happiness
What we pray stares at us
Whom we miss smiles at us

Zigzag can stop us from seeing
Obstacles can come in front of the eyes
Obduracy of human being brings the light
Multimedia zooms the eyes through miles

www.ingramcontent.com/pod-product-compliance
Lightning Source LLC
Chambersburg PA
CBHW060423050426
42449CB00009B/2099